Lea
t

by Kenneth E. Hagin

❧

CHAPTER 1

Learning What Short-Circuits the Power

When I came over among the Pentecostals, I learned that very few really understood the subject of faith. However, I didn't turn a deaf ear to them. I always listened to older ministers and to my elders, whether I agreed with them or not, because I had so much respect for them.

People will often "tune out" anybody they don't agree with. If they would listen, however, God might be able to teach them something through others.

So I would listen to my elders and to older ministers. That's one of the ways I learned as a young minister.

One important truth came to me from an older man who had been a Nazarene minister before he received the baptism of the Holy Spirit and began to pastor Pentecostal churches. In those days, Nazarenes would hold altar services where they'd pray to get "sanctified." They thought they received the baptism of the Holy Spirit by this experience of sanctification, which they called "the second definite work of grace."

After this brother preached, he normally prayed with the people until after midnight. After he came over among the Pentecostals, he often preached in open-air meetings. There were no public address systems in that day, and with the wind blowing, he'd have to lift his voice above all the other noise.

He would also pray for several hours in the afternoon, getting ready for his night service. He believed that "God wouldn't hear you unless you prayed loudly," so he prayed so loudly that people could hear him two or three blocks away. He nearly wore his voice out before the night service even started, and eventually his voice just quit on him altogether.

Because there was no air-conditioning in those days, in the afternoons this brother would carry a little canvas army cot outside and put it under a tree in the backyard. He'd lie there and pray to himself, very quietly, since by that time he had no voice left.

"I found out that you didn't have to do all that hollering," he said. "Man, you talk about getting anointed! I got more anointed and did more for God this way than I ever did when I was hollering all the time!"

What often happens is that *people feel the power, but then they short-circuit it by yelling or shouting*—and they think the yelling or shouting is the Holy Spirit. I saw this in dealing with Pentecostals, in particular.

I was holding a meeting in East Texas, and after one of the night services, as I was having a sandwich with the pastor and his wife, he had to leave the room to take a telephone call privately in his office. In his absence, I kept eating my sandwich and drinking my milk—and his wife kept saying, "My, my, Tsk, tsk, tsk. We're in for it now! My, my, my!"

I thought, *Dear Lord, what have I done?* Finally I said, "Sister, what is it? If it's me, I'll straighten it up!"

"Oh, Brother Hagin," she said, "was I talking out loud?"

"Yes."

She said, "I thought I was just talking to myself. I'm not talking about you."

I said, "If I'm doing something wrong, just tell me. I'll do right. I'll straighten it up."

Some may ask, "What if the Lord told you to do it?" I'm going to honor that man's office; he's pastor there. Remember David? Even though King Saul was wrong, David would not touch him. God said, ". . . *Touch not mine anointed, and do my prophets no harm*" (1 Chron. 16:22).

Why did I say this to the pastors? Because other people have the Holy Spirit besides us. They know when the Spirit is moving too. I wouldn't even go into another man's church and preach the faith message if that pastor didn't want me to! I've got plenty of other topics I can preach on that will bless and help the people.

I used to give congregations small doses of faith. It's like feeding babies: You can't feed babies beefsteak, corn bread, and onions. Babies can't even hold a glass of milk by themselves. You've got to spoon-feed them. Spiritually speaking, it's the same thing. Sometimes I would give them only one teaspoon full of faith in a two- or three-week meeting. Why? They weren't ready for it!

So the pastor's wife assured me that I hadn't done anything wrong. She explained that she was thinking of the woman her husband was counseling on the telephone. She said, "Brother Hagin, do you remember a certain woman who came to the altar to be saved tonight?"

"Yes," I said.

"Well," the pastor's wife continued, "her husband has been saved for years and has been a member of this church. He's a fine Christian, but she hasn't been living for the Lord. She came to the Lord last year, but she's been out of church now for many months. Tonight she came back to the Lord as a backslider. Tomorrow night, she'll come forward when you ask for those who want to be filled with the Spirit. And I'll tell you, she'll scream like a freight train going through a tunnel!"

Sure enough, the next night, I invited people to come to be healed and filled with the Spirit. About fifteen responded, including the woman the pastor's wife had told me about. I talked to her a little bit. After a few questions, I "located" her spiritually. She told me she had come back to God, and she wanted to be filled with the Holy Spirit.

I laid hands on her. The Holy Spirit came upon her—and she started screaming. It sounded like a freight train going through a tunnel! I looked at my watch. It was only 9:30, and I thought, *Well, it's early. It won't hurt for her to scream a little. I'll just let her go for a while.* So I went on down the line, laying hands on people. Out of the fifteen people in the line, about seven received the baptism of the Holy Spirit. After ministering to everyone in the line, I went back to this woman. Not only was she still screaming—now she was jerking, jumping, *and* screaming!

I laid my hands on her shoulders, shook her, and said, "Shut up!" I had to shout so she could hear me. "I command you to shut up in the Name of Jesus!" I shouted. She shut up.

I said, "Now open your eyes and look at me. That's the power of God that came on

7

you, all right—but *you're short-circuiting the power!* The Bible says, 'They were all filled with the Holy Ghost and began to *speak* with other tongues.' It doesn't say that they were all filled with the Holy Ghost and began to *scream.* Now, quit that screaming and start talking in tongues!"

As fast as you could snap your fingers, she started speaking in tongues fluently.

Often, people like her who are screaming, or are making funny noises, are short-circuiting the genuine power of the Holy Spirit. You may ask, "Is that the Holy Spirit?"

Yes and no. It's the Holy Spirit *on* them— but they're the ones reacting to the Spirit that way and short-circuiting the power. We're to do what the Scripture said to do with the power of the Holy Spirit: Let the power flow *through* us; not make a lot of noise when we feel the power.

There's also something we need to understand about messages in tongues in order to keep confusion out of our services.

1 CORINTHIANS 14:27

27 If any man speak in an unknown tongue, let it be by two, or at the most by three, and that by course; and let one interpret.

You're always safe scripturally to remain quiet once three persons have spoken. Don't join in by interpreting. (You could in the next service.) But *if something else needs to be said, one of those three should speak.*

Notice in this same fourteenth chapter, the Holy Spirit said through Paul, "*. . . God is not the author of confusion. . . .*" (v. 33), and "*Let all things be done unto edifying*" (v. 26). If *we* are the ones initiating some manifestation, it would not be edifying. So be sure you are acting under the anointing of the Holy Spirit. Then your actions will be edifying.

Some people just naturally have a shrill voice. If you're in that category, pray quietly. *Don't do anything that would attract attention to yourself and hinder other people from praying.* (If you're someplace alone, you can bray like a donkey if you want to!)

In Pentecostal circles, we used to close every meeting by coming around the altar and praying out loud. That was fine, but some people always wanted to pray at the top of their lungs. In almost every instance, *the overly loud people were short-circuiting the Spirit in the flesh.* Most of them wanted people to think they were really anointed, so they attracted attention to themselves "so everybody can see what I've got."

Everybody would be flowing with the Spirit, but one person would distract everybody with their loudness, and it stopped the flow of the Spirit. You don't have to be loud. God will hear you.

You pastors need to go to these people privately and correct them in love. Don't correct them publicly unless their behavior is really extreme.

But I can tell you ahead of time what they are going to tell you. Their excuse will be, "I can't *help* it!" I know, because I've dealt with them. In one of my meetings, a woman kept interrupting me as I was preaching. She tried to talk in tongues; she screamed; and she did other things. Her excuse was, "I can't help it. The Holy Ghost made me do it." But when the ushers carried her out, she cussed at them!

We need discernment in such cases. Notice this: Something is wrong when someone says, "I can't help it." (On the other hand, if someone were to say, I didn't *want* to help it," I'd accept that as the truth.)

When someone says, "I can't help it," I know right away that his actions were not inspired by the Holy Spirit—because the Holy Spirit never *makes* anybody do anything. He never uses force. (If He did, He would make everybody get saved today, and we'd go into the Millennium tomorrow.) The Holy Spirit only gives you a gentle push. Its demons and devils who *drive* and *force* people to do things.

Yes, there may be times when the Holy Spirit will seem to build up in you like steam, and you will think you're going to blow apart

11

if you don't do something. But if you're in the wrong place to let loose, get off by yourself. Otherwise, the unlearned in that church service will be injured and driven away from the things of God by your actions!

Why am I going into all this? Because we're going to have more and more outbursts of the flesh as we have greater and greater manifestations of the Holy Spirit. You need to know these things in order to stay on course.

CHAPTER 2

Learning to Interpret
the Flow

Now let's read the twenty-eighth verse of First Corinthians 14. There's a twofold meaning here, whether you realize it or not.

1 CORINTHIANS 14:28

28 But if there be no INTERPRETER, let him keep silence in the church; and let him speak to himself, and to God.

Notice Paul didn't say, "If there's no one present who can interpret." He didn't say, "If there is no one present with the interpretation of tongues." He said, *"If there be no INTERPRETER. . . ."*

I never understood it at the time, but after I was baptized in the Holy Spirit, no matter whose service I attended, I would always know which way the Spirit was going to move. God uses certain ones in this way as "interpreters." That's what I do in a lot of our services: I *interpret* which way the service is going, and I ask certain people, "Do you have something? Should you do this?"

You see, just because you may be used in *interpretation* of tongues does not make you an *interpreter*. I think there is a great deal more to "interpretation" than what we have seen.

Brother and Sister J.R. Goodwin had the best order I've ever seen in a church. Why? Because Brother Goodwin had trained his people. You pastors should train your people; they need to be taught correctly so they can be used of God.

In Brother Goodwin's church I saw a manifestation of the Spirit that I've never seen anywhere else, and I think most pastors would have missed it. They wouldn't have been spiritual enough to see it, but Brother Goodwin was a better "interpreter" of what God is doing.

There was a middle-aged woman in his congregation who had only gone to the second grade in school, so her reading ability was very limited. She had never read the Bible. She came to Brother Goodwin and said, "You know, sometimes in the service when we're singing or praising, or when you or someone else is preaching, something will say to me, 'Psalm 5:1 and 2, or Psalm 6 verse 3, the latter part of the verse.'"

I'm well satisfied that 999,999 out of a million Full Gospel pastors would have missed the genuine working of the Holy Spirit through her. But Brother Goodwin said to the woman, "The next time that happens, Sister, just lift your hand. If I think it is the right place, I'll recognize you, and you can give it out and we'll read the Scripture and see what it says. But if I don't recognize you, don't get your feelings hurt."

I've been in services when the Holy Spirit was moving a certain direction, and this woman would lift her hand. If Brother

Goodwin or I would recognize her—depending on who was preaching—she would repeat what she had heard, and when we read the Scriptures, or put them together, it was absolutely amazing: There was a message there, and the message was exactly the way the Holy Spirit was moving in that service.

Brother Goodwin allowed the woman to do that because he was an interpreter: *He interpreted the way the Holy Spirit was moving.* Not all pastors are that sensitive to the movings of the Spirit. I've preached for some who weren't, and when the Holy Spirit was trying to move, I've had to keep quiet, sitting there on the platform, because the dear pastor conducting the service wouldn't have recognized the Holy Spirit if He had come walking down the aisle with a red hat on!

But I didn't do or say anything, because the Holy Spirit is a gentleman; and if you're full of the Holy Spirit, you'll be a gentleman or a lady. (If I had taken over the service, I may have created more havoc than the pastor could

settle because of his inability to move in the Spirit.)

Now I want to share with you some thoughts about prophecy:

Prophecy is supernatural utterance in a known tongue. *Divers kinds of tongues* is supernatural utterance in an unknown tongue. *Interpretation of tongues* is a supernatural showing forth of that which has been said in tongues.

Prophecy is usually considered to be speaking by inspiration in one's own thoughts. However, when you speak by inspiration, the Holy Spirit will give you some new thoughts which you've never thought of. Sometimes it is a special utterance. So preaching the Word under the inspiration and anointing of the Holy Spirit is also prophecy.

Paul said in First Corinthians 14:31, *"For YE MAY ALL PROPHESY one by one, that all may learn, and all may be comforted."* Evidently this is what the first Christians did in their believers' meetings (we would call them church meetings).

A good testimony, anointed by the Holy Spirit, is similar to prophecy. Predicting the future, however, is *not* included in the simple gift of prophecy. To prophesy, Paul wrote in First Corinthians 14:3, is to speak unto men *". . . to EDIFICATION, and EXHORTATION, and COMFORT."*

You see, *there is a difference between prophesying and the ministry of a prophet.* You may all *prophesy,* as Paul said, but everyone is not a *prophet.*

CHAPTER 3

Learning to Control the Excesses

When I first came into Pentecostal circles in 1937, many Full Gospel churches had a testimony meeting every time they held a church service: *"For ye may all prophesy* [speak] *one by one. . . ."* My, the anointing was on some of those people! There is a real blessing and thrill in speaking under the inspiration of the Holy Spirit, and we ought to give everyone the opportunity to enjoy that blessing.

On the other hand, if the first person who testifies starts off with a hard luck story, everyone will try to top that story. For example, a woman once testified in one of my meetings, "The devil has been after me all the week, bless his holy name"—and then she went on to tell about all the troubles she had been having. Whenever that would happen in the churches

I pastored, I would get up and stop the meeting at that point and change the direction of the service (and that's what you pastors need to do when this happens in your services).

Testimony meetings have deteriorated through the years. Most testimony meetings today are really "backslidden" replicas of what Paul is talking about in First Corinthians 14:31. In only one of my pastorates was I ever able to develop the testimony meeting to the level it should be, by training the people and controlling the excesses.

I'll guarantee you this: As we move into this new wave of the Spirit, we're going to see more and more excesses or fanaticism, because *there are always excesses in any move of the Spirit.* You may as well get ready for it; you'll not have any move of the Spirit without excesses. Why? Because there will always be those in your midst who are unlearned.

In the so-called "Faith Movement" which God has raised up in recent years (I just call it the Word of God Movement), we've had all kinds of extremes. Dear Lord, people got off on all kinds of tangents. But that doesn't do away with the *real!*

We try to stay balanced and stay in the middle of the road. I tell my students that if they can't find where the Bible says something, they shouldn't say it either.

Some pastors claim that I endorse what they're doing in their churches—and I don't even know them. Others claim that I recommend their ministry—and I don't know them either. Still others claim that I agree with some manifestations of the Spirit which have supposedly taken place in their meetings. I'd have to be present in their meetings to know whether I agreed with these manifestations or not.

I remember one dear man who couldn't read or write—in fact, he wouldn't have known his name if it had been written on a neon sign four feet tall—yet God sometimes used him mightily in testimony meetings. I've seen a service that was just as dead as it could

21

be—until he'd get up and begin to testify under the anointing of the Holy Spirit.

Remember, Paul said, ". . . *ye may all prophesy one by one, that all may . . . be COMFORTED.*" And to prophesy is to speak "*. . . unto men to EDIFICATION, and EXHORTATION, and COMFORT.*" We were *edified.* As this man spoke, it felt like something went out over the whole crowd and blessed everybody! Oh, we got blessed!

However, in his unlearned state, this man would also make mistakes. I talked to him privately about them, and I was finally able to curb his actions a little without hurting his feelings.

Sometimes he would dance a little jig *in the Spirit* and everybody would get blessed. Then, the next time he came to church, he'd think to himself, *Well, let's see: Last time, I got up and said that and did this*—and he would stand up *in the flesh* and say the same thing in the same place and dance the same little step in the same place—and it just made everybody sick to their stomach! It wasn't any more in the Spirit than I'm an astronaut and just landed on Mars ten minutes ago.

When *God* moves, everybody will be blessed.

If something is of the *flesh*, everybody will have a sick feeling.

And if something is of the *devil,* it seems like the hair will stand up on your neck.

That's a simple way everyone can judge, whether they've got any spiritual discernment or not.

I'm convinced that every church ought to have believers' meetings from time to time, because many of these manifestations of the Holy Spirit won't occur when there are outsiders or sinners in a service.

In the days when I first came among Pentecostals, our largest services were on Sunday nights, when outsiders came. On Sunday mornings there was seldom anybody there but our own people, so I turned those Sunday morning services into believers' meetings. (In recent years when people's habits of church attendance have changed, the midweek service would probably be the most appropriate time for a believers' meeting.)

I would simply announce to the congregation, "Now, I'm going to sit down and turn this service over to the Holy Spirit. If you feel like you've got anything—an utterance in tongues, an interpretation, a prophecy—fine. If you feel like singing a chorus, just start singing. And if you feel like dancing, just get up and start dancing!"

There *is* a dance in the Spirit. We've got a substitute for it nowadays: It's that little kangaroo hop people do. Don't misunderstand me; I'm not minimizing it. It's all right in the right place, just like clapping your hands in the right place is all right. But it's one thing to dance *in the flesh* and another thing to dance *in the Spirit*. It's good to know which place is the right place. Most of the time, the majority of Charismatics are out of place.

We had a farmer in those services who never missed it when it came to dancing in the Spirit. We had no music. Everyone was sitting quietly. (Today, people have to have music before they can get into that kangaroo hop.)

1 CORINTHIANS 14:26

26 How is it then, brethren? when ye come together, every one of you hath a psalm . . . hath a tongue . . . hath an interpretation. . . .

Notice that Paul is not talking about the Corinthians going out and preaching when he said "when ye come *together*." Members of the Early Church did most of their evangelistic work out on the streets because they didn't have churches then; they met in homes.

So what Paul was talking about was what we'd call a believers' meeting. He said, "*every one of you hath a psalm . . . hath a tongue . . . hath an interpretation . . .*" (1 Cor. 14:26). The Corinthians went to church because they *had* something. People who *have* something still go to church; however, most people today go to church to *get* something.

So I'd tell my congregation, "I'm going to turn this over to the Holy Spirit now. Whatever you think you have, that's fine."

Somebody once asked, "Well, what if I miss it?"

I replied, "What of it? There's nobody here but us [believers]. It won't hurt anything."

You see, it *wouldn't* have been good if they had missed it in the evening service, when unlearned people and outsiders were present. That's where some of you miss it: You go to a church service and come across like a *storm*, exhibiting all kinds of fanatical behavior. And you do this in front of the unlearned and outsiders—people who are unsaved—so you do more harm than good!

A pastor told me about a man who came into his church and acted unwisely—with the result that the church split, and the pastor lost half his congregation. That's not right. I'd

26

certainly hate to have to meet God after messing up somebody's congregation!

"But God sent me," these people always say. No, God didn't send you to divide anybody's church! God told you to walk in love, and *love never divides*. We need to be very careful along these lines. A word of warning should be sufficient.

So I'd just sit down in our believers' meetings. The pianist would be at the piano (it was the only instrument we had). Sometimes the pianist would feel led to start a chorus, and sometimes somebody else in the crowd would start one, if they felt like it, and we'd all join in.

At other times, we would be sitting there in silence—no music, no nothing—and that farmer I mentioned would suddenly jump up and start dancing in the Spirit! Everybody got blessed. Then half the church jumped up and started dancing in the Spirit with him. Not one of them was dancing in the flesh.

And sometimes the Spirit of God would be so intense that *it felt like we were basking in the sunlight of heaven*. It felt like the very atmosphere was charged. Nobody said a word. There was just silence—holy silence—and we were almost afraid to move. It seemed like if we were to move, we'd destroy the atmosphere. Not a baby cried (we weren't able to have a nursery; it was a one-room church), and not a child moved. They sensed the same thing. We were just soaking this up, sitting in God's presence. We might sit that way for forty-five minutes. I think we once went as long as an hour and a half in silence. Glory to God! We need to learn about these things and experience them again.

The husband of one of our members was unsaved. He brought his wife to church on Sunday mornings, and then he went uptown to a place that wasn't supposed to be open on Sundays, but it was. He'd gamble and do other things until it was time to pick his wife up at church.

We'd start our morning worship service at 10:45, and sometimes we'd stay until 2:30 in the afternoon. But if the Spirit was not moving, I'd always dismiss at noon. (There was no use going on and on and on when God wasn't in it.)

One Sunday noon, this unsaved man drove up to the church, parked his car, rolled the windows down, but he couldn't hear a thing. He said later he even walked up to the windows of that little frame building, but because the windows were painted over—we didn't have stained glass—he couldn't see inside. He actually put his ear up against the window.

He told us later, "I thought, *Well, I know they're here. All their cars are in the parking lot, but I can't hear anything. Do you suppose the Rapture has taken place?*" (He'd once been in a service where the minister had preached on "the catching away," or Rapture.) The man returned to his car, waited a while longer, still didn't hear anything, and went back to the window to listen again. We were still sitting in holy silence.

Finally the man opened one of the church doors and stepped inside. The church was two-thirds full, but everybody was just sitting there. I was sitting on the platform. Nobody was saying a word. After looking around, he sat down on the end of the back pew. I watched him. Nobody said a word.

After the man had sat there about ten minutes, he suddenly started to shake all over, like he had chills. Then, still shaking, he got up from the pew, walked down to the front of the church, fell across the altar bench, and called on God. And nobody even went down there to pray with him: We all just sat there. I decided, *God started it; let Him finish it!* (Often when God starts something and we try to finish it, we get into a mess.)

Some of the most marvelous things I've ever seen in my life happened in those believers' meetings. God intended it to be that way: Every believer should have the privilege of

30

operating under the anointing and gaining experience in exercising the gifts of the Spirit in services where nobody will be harmed by their mistakes.

I'm teaching more explicitly about these matters than I ever have. The reason is because God is endeavoring to get us ready for the move of His spirit that is ahead of us. (In fact, we're already in that move to a certain extent.)

However, I've been in the ministry long enough to know that the same problems recur in every mighty move of God. Some people always go to the extreme—into excess and fanaticism—and this causes some ministers to back off from *all* manifestations of the Holy Spirit—and I can understand their position.

There is a very fine line between real spirituality on the one hand, and fanaticism and excess on the other hand. The two can be so close that sometimes it's difficult to distinguish or discern between them.

Although I am not in favor of excess, I've said for years that I'd rather have a little wild-fire and God moving than no fire at all! I'd rather have a little excess and fanaticism than have the order of a graveyard, with nothing happening!

Anytime there is a move of God and things are happening, there will always be those who will go to excess. However, if these people are honest and sincere, they will accept correction—and we'll get that power channeled in the right direction, where it will make tremendous power available, dynamic in its working.